T0127707

Bruised
but
Not Broken

U. R. WORTHY

authorHOUSE®

AuthorHouse™
1663 Liberty Drive
Bloomington, IN 47403
www.authorhouse.com
Phone: 1 (800) 839-8640

© 2018 U. R. Worthy. All rights reserved.

No part of this book may be reproduced, stored in a retrieval system, or transmitted by any means without the written permission of the author.

Published by AuthorHouse 03/19/2018

ISBN: 978-1-5462-3025-0 (sc)
ISBN: 978-1-5462-3023-6 (hc)
ISBN: 978-1-5462-3024-3 (e)

Library of Congress Control Number: 2018902349

Print information available on the last page.

Any people depicted in stock imagery provided by Getty Images are models, and such images are being used for illustrative purposes only. Certain stock imagery © Getty Images.

This book is printed on acid-free paper.

Because of the dynamic nature of the Internet, any web addresses or links contained in this book may have changed since publication and may no longer be valid. The views expressed in this work are solely those of the author and do not necessarily reflect the views of the publisher, and the publisher hereby disclaims any responsibility for them.

Table of Contents

In memory of the Life of Markeisha

She looked in the mirror after a deep awakening. Noticing someone who resembled her but, had never been seen before. It was beauty, it was grace, it was resilience. You see she had always seen weakness and hurt, pain and regret, shame and guilt. Abandon by those sworn to love her and storing up deep rooted pain of worthlessness and dissolutions of what her perception of love was.

You see her life had been filed with fragments of unhealthy examples. Those who modeled the picture where actors playing the parts they were given by their guides, the ones who came before her. It's a cycle you see, generational curses, carrying the torch for cycles of ill will, ill love. Burdens which came with pardons that would cleanse the palette of those who wish to break chains that hold them captive to what once was, and still is a force that should not continue.

You see, she realized something that pain she held on to, it was a disguise. One she'd clothed herself in, too ashamed to walk in her truth. Too ashamed to confront the real her inside. What would happen if she cried out? Not the cry for others pain, but the pain she never grieved. You see, her pain was not a worthy cause. She'd taken up the touch, to run into battles for those whose voices where never heard. But what about her voice? Can you hear her? Would you hear her?

Empty from the cries she'd let out before, praying for a rescue that would never came. When would someone help fight her battles? This woman, a girl trapped inside of an empty shell praying for sweet nectar to quince the thirst of the bitterness she'd been fed her whole life. When will it come? Who would come?

Instead she rises from her salted wounds waiting for the cavalry. This time she stands, not for a cause, not for others but for a queen who has write-fully returned to her throne. Your majesty, your worth, it is an honor to finally meet you!

INTRODUCTION

This book is based on the live of a woman who struggles her whole life trying to find her. Dealing with countless setback while battling depression she refused to be a victim of her circumstance and joined the military as way out the streets.

Finding true love and hoping that she would finally see herself as "worthy" she set out to become the best wife and mother she could. It was then life threw curve ball and as she faced issues of abandonment after the loss of her marriage.

Fighting a losing battle with depression while searching for her lost identity was she able to find her healing and overcome it all.

Dedicated to My King in the making

The happiest day of my life was becoming your mother. From the moment I looked in your big brown eyes I fell in love with you and I made a promised to God and you that I would protect, love and guide you to my very last breath. Knowing that I'm not perfect I look to you in my times of weakness. Its then that you give me strength, encouragement and more wisdom than a child should ever possess.

These last few years have been tough watching me go through my depression but as a young king you rose to the occasion and gave me a will to go on. You are the best thing that could have ever happened to me.

Thank you for saving my life, My king in the making.

Love Always momma

CHAPTER 1

Growing Up

Growing up, we always had to share everything. Having four girls, hand me-downs was like going to the mall for us. We lived in public housing all our lives and this time we had a 3-bedroom house. So, you do the math it wasn't huge, but it was just right for us.

With my sisters I never really felt like I was special. Like I stood out. The oldest she was smart, and gorgeous with long hair. Then there was me short hair ok grades, but I never saw myself as the pretty one. The younger two only 11 months apart and they were just the cutest little girls ever who could do no wrong. My baby sister would come my senior year of high school.

My father worked for many years and retired. He wasn't very involved with our day to day life. He spent most his days in our basement drinking and getting high with his friends. I have a few fond memories I hold dear of him, but most are overshadowed by the many days and nights he would beat my mother or sister.

It was very common for a parent or family member to have an addition problem. Honestly, I didn't realize it was an issue until I got older and understood that it was an epidemic. Some families didn't have dads, and at least mines was still around in some capacity.

My mother worked as a nursing assistant in a nursing home and she was very passionate about her work. All her patients loved and adored her. I remember visits to my mother's job and her patients would brag on her as if she was their child.

The family members of the patients really respected her and during the holidays they would buy her gifts and give her cards with large amounts of cash in it just to say how much they appreciated her.

It was that same love my mother brought to the neighborhood. She was like everybody's "big momma" or auntie always willing to help someone out in need. Heck if you ask my sisters they'd say we were the ones in need, but you'd never know it.

One of my earliest memories growing up was that of my mother helping someone in their time of need. I remember she used our rent money to rent a U-Haul to pick up a family member and her kids because they had fell on hard times. This would happen quite often.

Whenever people would come to stay with us and they were all welcomed with opened arms. Over the years aunts, uncles, cousins and neighborhood friends graced our doors steps. It was during those years of watching my mom caring for people I knew that I wanted to be that type of person who cared for people.

Chapter 2

Take Care of Home

Some might read this and say, "you're supposed to help family "but I'd say, "you're supposed to take care of home first" and there were times where my sisters and I felt like we were the guest in our own home and had overstayed our welcome.

With mom working all the time that left us kids usually to fend for ourselves or left in the care of whoever was willing to keep us, and my dad was usually consumed with his drugs and friends to ever even know we were there.

As a child you aren't allowed to voice your opinion. When we had family living with us we had no say in giving up our rooms, sometimes sleeping two to a bed. At times guest mistreated us, rationing the food our mother brought. My mother was too busy working or trying to help someone to realize what was happening under her own roof.

You would think as a mother of girls at some point talks of self-worth, boys and other notions would be spoken of but that wasn't true in my house. The lack of conversation caused a void for us girls not ever really feeling worthy.

CHAPTER 3

Bruised

I think I was about 8 or 9 and I was home alone with one of those family members my mother was trying to help when he pinned me down and started to kiss me. I told him to stop, and he told me he was doing me a favor that I was so ugly no one would take my virginity anyway. I cried a little, but I stopped fighting and let him have his way.

Never said anything about it because who would believe me? He was right no one wanted me, so I thought. He had done some things to me before and I told his mother and she whooped me for "being fast" so I learned to be quiet.

You would think as a mother of girls at some point talks of self-worth, boys and other notions would be spoken of but that wasn't true in my house. I know that my mother told me that I was beautiful, but I can't say that was a regular conversation we had.

With my sisters I never felt like I was special. Like I stood out. The oldest she was smart, and gorgeous with long hair. Then there was me short hair ok grades, but I never saw myself as the pretty one and after my rape I remember telling myself no one would think I was beautiful. The younger two only 11 months apart and they were just the cutest little girls ever who could do no wrong.

I never had the courage to tell my mother about my rape but, some years later at a family member's house the unthinkable would happen. I remembered being touched, forced to do things I shouldn't have and this time I told my mom and she promised she'd fix it. I came home to find my mother and an adult family member waiting for me to arrive from school. They told me how I must've been confused and made the story up. They convinced me that it would kill my father if he knew.

Confused, hurt I ran to my room and cried. My mother, my champion? She's not fighting for me? How could she? She didn't know how to fight. She had been abused for so long by my father that she had no clue how to stand.

CHAPTER 4

What Worth?

Over the years we'd frequent battered woman shelters just to be safe only to return to him after a few days. After a brutal beating one day, he come down the stairs a walked out the door closely followed by my sister. Furious because of all the beatings our mother took she picked up a big crystal punch bowl and threw it out the door at him.

Frantically locking the door, we screamed for my mother to save us from whatever madness he would return to do. Sure, enough he enters the house goes straight for my sister trying to hurt her, but mother stood in between them. He picked up a stroller and began to beat her with it. My mother's screams were so loud, crying from the pain.

She suffered a broken arm, and ribs black eyes and swollen lips. When I tried to call the police her response," no he didn't mean it"

You see these are just a few things that shattered my worth before it reached its true value. Bruised me and gave me scares that I never truly healed from.

CHAPTER 5

Broken

At the age of 13 my body began to change. I grew curves and breast and the attention started to come my way from older guys. A neighbor's brother, he was so fine in my eyes. Light skinned, pretty eyes and muscles for days. And he wants me?

This is a dream that I'm surely going to wake from. After a brief introduction from his niece we began to talk over the phone. Knowing that he was older I told him I was 16 and he in turn said that he was 19. We spent hours on the phone talking. This man made me feel good about myself. A girl with no sense of self-worth or self-esteem it was easy for me to love him. For once I felt special and wanted.

Sharing my dreams to join the military, he instantly responded with you will have my children one day. Silly me, thinking this was an honor he wants me to have his child? I conceded to the idea for a while and quickly realized that I didn't want it to be my reality.

The first time we had sex I didn't know what to do or what he was doing. I cried having flashes of when I was raped. That word "rape" it holds so much power. It traps it's capture in a cell of deceit, shame, hurt and lies making you want to crawl in a corner and just hide.

The lack of love that I had for myself cause me to continue to make poor judgement calls, no protection and hooking school to say the least and when I did wise up to get some birth control it was too late. It was about 3 am and I woke up vomiting and cramping bad. I went to my mother and she just told me to lay down it would go away. An hour later the ambulance had to be called for all the pain.

When we arrived, I remember them separating me from my mother. The nurse said your 13 and your pregnant if you don't tell your momma I will! At this time my older sister had come when she heard what happened. They let her in to talk to me first and my mom burst in the door. What's wrong? You bet not tell me your pregnant! What will people think of me if you are pregnant? You're not keeping it!

My sister held me as I wept in her arms out of fear and shame that I had angered my mother and let my dreams die all because this guy said I was pretty. We got back home from the hospital only for my mother to separate me from my sister. She was angry because she overheard her tell me words of encouragement.

My sister devised a plan. We can do this together, she

said. Due any day now and figured we'd take shifts with the kids so that she could finish college and I high school.

My mother forbids her to see me and asked her to leave.

Mother told me "this is on me, my sin, your only 13. You will have an abortion because I'm not having this shit". She'd demand information about the father, but I refused to give her any. She left me alone in the dark to cry swearing me to secrecy afraid that the discovery of my pregnancy would tarnish her image.

It was the 4th of July momma worked a double and I caught a cab to see him. Unable to reach me my mother tracked me down using the cab company the next morning. To everyone's surprise including mines he was 24years old, he had lied to me about his age too! To save her honor she pressed charges on him for statutory rape and schedule my abortion. I cried the whole time before and after the procedure. Depression began a normal thing for me at this time.

Close to our court date collect calls started to come. Not for me but for my mother. She made a deal with the child's father that if the charges were dropped he'd pay her $500 and she agreed. The day came, we sat in the courtroom and she pulled the prosecutor aside to talk. I remember the feeling that feeling it felt like my honor had been sold. I know I had sex with him consensually but when she pressed charges it felt like she was finally standing for me. My champion had finally arrived. She was standing firm on her belief that this was wrong.

Although I didn't agree that because of the lies the father and I both told my mother was trying to protect me in her own way. Feelings short lived, the charges were dropped, and he never paid her a dime.

When I look back at my childhood I have more questions than memories. Roadblocks that I have put up on my head trying not to remember things that have

happened to me only for them to return as nightmares.

So, the question is, did I grow up? Hell did I ever even

have a chance?

Chapter 6

Navy Days

During my high school years my family suffered more than ever. The loss of a nephew which tore my sister apart and the subsequent realization that my mother had developed her own addiction the resulted in the loss of her job. This stressed me even more feeling like the weight of the world has seemingly been placed on my shoulders.

Taking a job as a live-in babysitter for a family friend to help bring in some money would be the beginning of something great for me. Unlike my house this woman constantly talked to me about my hopes and dreams. She encouraged me to join the military and get out the city. Friend to my mother and witnessing he downfall was evidence enough to know that things weren't the same.

Spending most my free time in JROTC classes I knew the military was my only way out and convinced myself that I could make enough money to come back and save my family. Passing a practice test with a recruiter one day we talked about the possibilities for me.

Navy's standards I was overweight by about 20lbs and he made a vow that he would work with me daily until I left for boot camp and he did. I'd wake up early and run in the mornings and he would pick me up afterschool to run in the evenings.

For months this was my daily routine. My recruiter had become one of my biggest supports. Rooting me on every step of the way. When it came down to choosing a job for the military the only thing I wanted to know, was when can I leave? Meeting my graduation requirements,

I remember trying to convince my mother to let me leave without the ceremony. She refused saying she wanted to see me walk the stage only to miss that very thing.

Six days after high school graduation I joined the United States Navy at the age of 17. This was best decision I'd ever made.

CHAPTER 7

Love At first sight

Being in the Navy people always joke about ship-life being the hook up spot. Can't say that was the case for me though. That wasn't really the case for me, however I did date once or twice until I found my husband.

Almost three years my junior and new to the ship he was sent to work for me in the Mess Hall. Not to sound cheesy but there was something there from day one. Smooth dark skin, muscled frame and one of the brightest smiles I had ever seen. When we met for the first time it was like we had known each other for an eternity.

We laughed, we joked and flirted all the time making the hours and days fly by.

One night the whole staff decided to go for dinner and drinks. It was about twelve of us all having a great time but somehow, he and I were in a world of our own. Talks of family, friend and hometown stories. It was like a serious episode of speed dating. We tried to learn as much about each in this rare outing.

Riding with a friend he was stranding and caught a ride with me home. We stayed up for hours talking, laughing about any and everything. His laugh was so infectious and easy to love. This would be the start of a world-wind romance.

After that night we spent every day together, sneaking around afraid that our coworkers would find me out about our secret love affair. One week turned into one month and by the second month we were madly in love with each other.

He'd told his mother about me and how he wanted to make me his wife. Sitting at the chili bar at work he asked me to marry him and I said yes. We planned to be married before deployment and his family came to support us. At the justice of peace with butterflies in my stomach I became the love of my life's wife.

We had only been together in total two and half months and my friends and family all thought we were crazy, but the love we had for each other was real and we didn't want to wait. The day we married was the best day of my life aside giving birth to my son.

My husband was a good man, he didn't smoke or drink, he was a good provider and he was always making sure my needs were meet. Shortly after we married I was deployed for seven months and it strained our new union. The distance for us was a huge problem. Making us insecure and unsure of our decision to marry so quickly. We barely knew each other.

Briefly meeting extended family and exchanging childhood stories were not enough to get us through this tough time. Returning from deployment he was standing on the pier with a dozen red roses and his family by his side and all was forgotten. Home at last.

We could finally start to build our lives as husband and wife. Learning to love more and more each day growing and maturing as a couple started to come with ease. We decided to start planning for the next chapter of our life and looked for a home. It would only take a few months searching and we brought our first home.

CHAPTER 8

Happily Ever After

Loving our new home, the mounting bills from our new responsibilities brought a new set of marital problems for us. It seems that each time we jumped one huddle two more would show up, but we always managed to make it in the end.

Every marriage has its ups and downs, but our downs seemed like anthills compared to most. Most of our issues stemmed from financial issues trying to juggle the cost of a new car with a large mortgage and was very stressful. It wasn't long before I fell ill at work ending up at the emergency room. It was Valentine's Day and I couldn't figure out what was wrong with me. The nurse enters my room and says, "congratulations you're going to be a mom"

Shocked and scared I didn't know how to react. Here it is my marriage is already rocky and now we're going to add a baby? The nurse cautioned me to take it easy due to some hemorrhaging. My pregnancy was detected very early on and it didn't look like the odds were in our favor adding extra stress.

Returning home late that night to a sleeping husband with candy and roses on the dresser waiting for me. He awoke from my return and saw the tears in my eyes asking what's wrong. Scared of the reaction he would give I paused, "I'm pregnant but, I might lose it." He reached for me and gave me a strong embrace. Rubbing my belly and whispering in my ear, we're going to be ok he's going to make it"

That night for the first time in my life I remember

feeling safe right there in his arms. It's hard to explain I knew he loved me, swore to protect me but right then in that moment I felt it. As the months past, my pregnancy suffered several complications.

At the beginning of my second trimester my doctor place me on strict bed rest and with our new addition coming my husband started to go on short deployments to bring in extra money. Whenever he wasn't gone he was always there for every appointment, foot rub, back message and random mood swings.

My husband the man who was growing before my eyes had turned into a great father long before the birth of our child. I remember arguing with him being pregnant and to escape I would jump in my car and speed off. One night after my temper tantrums he was waiting for me at the door. With a mellow tone he told me, "it's my duty to protect you and my son and if you feel like you need to leave I will because I can't bear the thought of losing you"

Stuck in my ways it was something I needed to think about. Growing up when arguments happened in our house it was usually a fight that would soon follow. I promised myself as an adult I would leave before that happened to me. Sitting quietly in the dark thinking about how I could explain this to the man I loved I decided I needed to change.

Almost two years into our marriage there were so many demons I hid from him hoping I would never have to face them again. We eventually talked about my fears and he assured me that he would never abuse me in any way. The tantrums still came but now I was quarantined to my house for their duration.

That's the kind of relationship we had. We fused but at the first sight of a smile the argument was over, and all was forgiven. He had my heart and I had his.

We welcomed our son in the fall of 2007 and the pride he had as he held him words can't explain. My husband loved being a father and made sure that my time as a new mother was worry free outside of nursing and dirty diapers. Our family wasn't perfect, but it was perfect for us.

Military careers, house, car and the kid we were happy. Taking on an extra responsibility of my sister my husband welcomed the idea with open arms and our family grew from 3 to 4 overnight.

Chapter 9

New Chapter

In 2010 I discharged from the Navy and started school full time shortly afterwards my husband received word that he would be a part of the navy's downsizing efforts. So, our family went from two working incomes to none in a matter of months. Stress began to mount remembering the days when money cause so many issues for us in the past.

My husband joined the ranks of college student hoping to generate some cash flow until work came. He focused on becoming a merchant seaman in hopes of seeing the world while he provided for us. Both taking classes at night and looking for work during the day it was a ritual for us. It's funny what started out as being stressful and threatened to tear us apart actually brought us together. We were closer than ever before.

We studied together, traveled and were more in love than ever before. Unemployment began to run out and tensions starting to rise just as he accepted a position and we were excited for a new chapter in our lives.

Our first goodbye was the hardest we had spent every day together for the last several years and now he was going away for four months. Signing my son up for every sport known to man, I prayed it would help pass the time. Before we knew it, he was home again. He spent a few weeks in and then off he went back to water. It was tuff on my son and I because we had such a close family.

My son would leap for joy any time he would hear his dad's voice they shared such a wonderful bond. I'd never witness a man in the household before especially not in this aspect. My father was around but didn't involve himself in our lives.

Now my husband wanted to know how his son's day went, who his friends were and told him constantly how much he loved him. This was one of the many qualities that made me love him even more.

Eventually I accepted a position with the government and it seemed as if we would recover financially. One day, working as a dietary aid I became injured. There was a popping noise and a tremendous amount of pain. Scheduled to deploy at weeks end my husband was worried about health. The morning of his departure I climbed out of bed only to fall to the floor. My whole left side had gone numb. Frantic seeing the pain I was in my husband tried to devise a plan to stay home.

Assuring him that I would be fine we left for the airport. He made me promised that if anything happened

I would send an emergency message for him to return him. After receiving my MRI results there was an emergent need for me to see a neurosurgeon.

My consultant with doctor was my husband's biggest fear. The doctor urging me to undergo surgery within the next few hours. Barely enough time to contact my family I decided to hold off on worrying my husband. Looking back now I can see how selfish it was of me to take that opportunity from him. The right to know that his wife's life was on the line and the right to be by her side. I thought that by not telling him, I was being strong for our family.

As I awoke from surgery my sister had called everyone in my contacts trying to get word back to him. He called, excited that I was ok but disappointed in the decision I made not to include him. "I'm coming home now" I told him not to worry that I would be fine. My mother had jumped on a bus and was set to arrive in a couple hours.

Weeks of physical therapy, countless follow up visits to put me on the road to recovery. Off from work due to my injury, I decided to fly out to Rome to see him.

It was the honeymoon we never had. The week was filled with tourist attractions and attempts to make another child.

Months flew by and it was time for his assignment to end but he wanted to stay longer. Trusting his judgement, I supported his decision. In the months that followed things started to change the calls were less frequent and time seem to be adding instead of subtracting. The calls that we did receive vaguely reminded us of the person he was.

CHAPTER 10

D-DAY

I remember it like it was yesterday. I had 7 Months and, in the days, leading up to his return it seemed like something was off. The calls became more frequent and far between. When they would come it seemed like it was being forced.

My son and I drove to the airport to pick my husband up and from the moment I felt like it was a stranger. His eyes looked cold and empty. What's wrong I asked tears flood his eyes? His reply was nothing. He hugged and kissed me, did the same for our son but this was different from all the other homecomings we'd hide this one felt forced, and unwanted. People always say I wear my emotions on my face and I couldn't quite understand until I saw it from someone else.

The whole ride home I asked repeatedly what's wrong? Are you ok? His response always the same," I'm just tired. We arrived home like we've done so many times before but this time it almost felt like I was being a stranger into my house.

The look in his eyes when I saw him. I couldn't shake it. It was shame, it was grief, it was pain. But why does the love of my life feel this way. On the months leading up to his return we started planning to renew our vows. The wedding we always dreamed of and it was coming soon. But that warm feeling inside, that undeniable love I knew my husband had for me had gone away and I had no clue what happened to it.

People asked me did you see the signs? Did you guys

argue? Did you do something wrong to him? And all my answers were no. Sure we had some ups and downs in our marriage but not now, not in the years prior it was some of our happier years. We laughed, we loved, we went to school together. Took trips and had some of the best times ever in the months leading up to this.

As he seemed to settle in to our routine a cooked dinner, he unpacked, and we sat down as a family for dinner and the table fell quiet. My concern grew deeper. When night ended he insisted that my son sleep with us because he missed him. As a mother I couldn't deny him that but as I wife I wanted my intimacy too. It had been so long since he held me in his arms. I felt like if I could just lay with him in his arms, connect with him, maybe these feeling would disappear.

Each night that followed resembled that of this one. The days we long he looked so out of place like he didn't want to be here.

My questions grow more increasingly and with that he became defensive and emotionally abusive. I had never seen this side of him! Not in the 10 Years we shared as husband and wife. The question I neglected to ask is the one I didn't want answered. Is there someone else? Playing it over and over in my head before I eventually asked. "Is their someone else?" He replied, "No" and the conversation ended just as quickly as it started.

Crying all night still unable to understand what was happening to the man I loved. Not the man who had always loved and respect me what is going on with him? In the months to come he became more distant. The signs were obvious to others, just not to me.

One day in a heated argument he told me it was over, and he wanted a divorce. Cancel the wedding! I want out. Those words crushed me. Crushed me to my soul, the core. I had been in love with this man since the first day we met. He was it for me just like I thought I was it for him.

We had grown together crossing over to different eras in adulthood as a strong force to be reckoned with. We made it through military deployments, first time home buyers, the complicated birth of our son and a couple failed attempts, to both being unemployed and trying our hand at college for the first time but we always made it through.

Now, him with his dream job traveling the world again and I with a government job. It was blessings on top of blessings. But somehow things went sour. The word "divorce" was the only word left for us.

He got a unit a few hours away and I was determined to make my marriage work even though I didn't know what was wrong. Driving down for the weekend, praying for a miracle to save us. Only to arrive to a cold shoulder.

He grabbed our son and the bags and walked right past me.

He took the next day off to spend time with my son and I stayed behind only to find foreign voicemails on his hotels phone. Maybe it's someone he works with calling the states, but at 3am? The next night he jumped up to take a call same time even walked out the room.

When questioned about the calls he said it was all in my head just someone calling from work.

Knowing I needed to get to his phone to put my fears to rest I asked for it. Something I had never been denied in 10 years and he told me no! It was then that I know it was another woman. I went home driving up the highway crying the whole way. Praying my son didn't ask to many questions because I had no answers.

He returned home a few months later and had received a new phone and I needed one too, so I asked to check out the features. Hesitantly, he complied right after he put the phone on silent. After quick thinking I put the phone on vibrate and not a second later a message came through. "Mi amour, just placed minutes on my phone call me when you leave her" I flipped through the phone. How could you? Reading the message aloud. You made me think it was me? Like I did something wrong? Got fat! Turned you off! Didn't love you enough and you were cheating the whole time! Screaming I hate you I told him to leave my house.

My mother was here at the time and had no clue what I was going through. To everyone else we were still the happy couple who just had to postpone the wedding. My mother flew down the stairs to ask questions and to her dismay my marriage was over, one that never seem to alert to any troubles before.

She talked with him trying to understand. He swore that it was a mistake and he didn't want to lose me. For weeks I had been trying to save a marriage he didn't want but after I found out about the cheating he screamed how much he loved me. I asked him a question tears streaming down my face "so you want her?" His reply, "I want you both" furious not sure from his new-found desire for truth or for the actual act.

Searching for months, knowing something was wrong and out of place. Should I feel vindicated? I don't! I feel defeated, ashamed and hurt. But my love for him was real and deep no questions about that. I decided to give it another try laying some demands at his feet. I forbid him to go back to that assignment telling him how I couldn't trust him with her around. He argued that he had no control of his duty assignments. Little did I know for months he had been trying to get his detailer to send him back there.

CHAPTER 11

Who is She?

The voicemails and text messages never left my mind. Who is she? Could she be someone he works with? Yeah. That's it, he works with her. I spent nights and days on social media looking at every girl that liked his pictures or pictures he'd liked. He had given my son his old phone to play with and with my mind going a hundred miles an hour I wondered if I could find any information leading me to her.

Retrieved the phone from my son only to find there was no SIM card. The phone calls weren't erased finding countless calls to his detailer. In the search engine was directions for a downtown hotel. Sleepless, anxious and desperate I needed answers, so I continued to social media looking for clues and there she was! A picture of a girl looking out the window of a famed Norfolk hotel with a caption "left my love in the USA" all these pictures my husband had liked.

Backtracking in my mind the dates, the times? Where was he? Where was I? During that timeframe he told me that his ship had suffered an oil spoiled and everyone had to stay onboard. Not realizing that he was laying up in the hotel with this woman all while I thought he was at sea.

After some magnum P.I detective work I found the woman name and number She had a name. I knew who she was and where to find her. His demeanor had changed, he became evil to me, distant and lacked affection. accusing me of being with someone else because after all, I had no proof at this point just accusations.

Here's a number. Its international and it's called all the time. On my way to work with my stomach tied in knots I decided to make the call.

Hello, the woman answered with a tremor in her voice" How are you? This is U. R. Worthy. The phone fell silent. I took a deep breath and exhaled, I'm not calling for drama, but I have questions and I need answers. She told me that I was confused it wasn't her that I was looking for but her best friend who was in a relationship with my husband. My response, "listen if that's what you want to say then give her my number and have her call me."

She paused. Ok, I'm sorry I am the one you want! But I never knew he was married. Instantly all I could see was the color red. Rage, anger, pain, grief every emotion you could think of. Was I ready for these answers? The things she would tell me I was never ready for. "She asked what do you want to know? I will tell you everything". She told me about their introduction and how she grew to love him over the course of months spent together. She swore that it wasn't until he was about to return to the states that she found out he was married.

I asked so why did she come to the states after knowing? You knew then he was married by then! There was a deep pause, "wait how did you know?" Angry more than I ever was before with my patience running short. I'd felt sorry for her before thinking she was the victim of another man's lies but knowing about me took me to another level of crazy.

Stop! You know what? Do you still have contact with him I asked? She promised that part of her life was over and that they were friends. Standing my ground and staking my claim, demands were made. You are not to contact my husband again. At this point I was furious.

Ending that call and dialing another, my husband was about to explain the new details that were given to me. Little did I know he was on the phone with her!

My calls and text went unanswered as my temper flew sky high.

When you are married to someone for a long time you tend to know passwords, pins and codes. Never thought I'd have to use them until a tiny voice in my head told me to check his voicemail. There were several messages all from her reporting back to him my every word I said as well as hers.

In one message she told him that she didn't tell me about the babies, dropping my phone mid message. What babies? What damn babies? This is just too much!

Of course, I was upset to say the least and I made the mistake of letting him know that I had the access code to his voicemail. He found a way to turn it all on me. Saying that I would never be able to forgive him, and I would never give our marriage a fighting chance bringing up old issues. Wait, what just happened? He convinced me that it was the past and I should leave it there. Like a good wife I hushed up and allowed him to place me back in the corner all over again like I was the one at fault.

Now at work, I sat at my desk with this numbness inside. Have you ever heard of the saying be careful what you ask for? I really wasn't ready for what just happened to me. It's real now! She exists! She's real! It's not in my head. It wasn't in my head.

That day at the airport, the look in his eyes it was the guilt eating him alive. He had been living a double life and the one he left behind was the one he wanted. I remember telling myself see, "you weren't crazy" it was then that you recognized the signs you just didn't want to believe it.

Hearing about the when and where's was just too much. I sunk into my chair wishing I could be anywhere but work to wrap my mind around this information.

Traveling to see him in August just months before is when they started dating. How could he!!!! Man, those emotions were so powerful. I could kill him, her too!!! She told me that he never spoke of me only our son. It wasn't until she came across our pictures that she began to ask questions. When confronted he told her we were over a long time ago and the only contact was for my son's wellbeing.

The woman told me she had stopped talking to him for a while but loved him.

My thoughts, were this is too much to deal with. At the end of our conversation she asked if she could have asked if I would answer a question for her. Yes, I replied. "What will you do with this information now?" I don't know, I love him, he's my husband and the father of my child and I want him, but I don't know right now." In my mind over in over that last response replayed.

Not being productive at all I left work crying and upset. Talking on the phone about our issues, I decided I was going to fight for my marriage once again. He was away again and this time I was going to make him remember the love we had. Packed the car and hit the road. I didn't tell him I was coming with the hopes that I would catch him red handed and somehow be convinced that I didn't want this anymore.

Knocked on the door and he pulled me close. Wait what is this? Passionate kisses. Could this be a new chapter for us? Did I just need those answers? He got in the shower, realizing old habits die hard I darted for his phone. He will not lie to me again, I thought.

Searching frantically hoping I'm not caught just in case there's nothing here to see. To my surprise I saw unread messages from her. My heart smiled for a minute. I can't lie a sense of calm and relief had come over me.

Being a fighter comes naturally when the odds are stacked against you, but there are times when you are up on the ropes waiting to give up and this was my moment. My life was a never-ending fight in my home, in school, but I never thought I would be fighting for my marriage. From my perspective, things were starting to turn around for us. In love for the moment until things fell apart again.

The calls started to come in more regularly. Flowers and candy for my anniversary and soon he'd be home for a while. His return was long awaited. Only home for a few weeks his behavior seemed very odd. Not wanting to cause a scene I shelved my feeling once again.

It seemed as if he was ready to leave just as quickly as he came. Checking his email daily for orders as lay in confusion.

At work on my way to lunch his car starts to follow me. Stopping grateful to see him, my eyes zoomed in on an envelope in his had one I knew all too well. That same look in his eye tells me he's going back to her.

CHAPTER 12

No Deeper Pain

Are you kidding me? No, I'm not dealing with this if you leave I want a divorce! I can't trust you! He replied, I understand. Wait? This is what you wanted? You want me to give you a divorce? No, I must go, its work, he responded.

Heart broken into pieces. I wanted to believe that his return was only to work but my gut said differently. This feeling, it's the same as before something's not right. At home he began packing for his trip and I cried as I looked on. Nothing could give me comfort. My heart told me if he got on that plane I would lose him forever.

When are you leaving? With a cold look in his eyes he said Monday. It's Friday? I know I just found out. I stormed out the house ended up at a bar drinking. So many thoughts, so many emotions, I can't think right now. I returned home intoxicated looking for a fight. He tried to console me. Shelter my feelings from the storm but it was too late. I was already consumed by my emotions.

Why won't you fight for us? I cried repeatedly. Trying to reassure of his commitment to his family he kept saying "it's just work".

The day came in we were at the airport. Unable to even make eye contact with me he focused all his attention to our son. Telling him about the adventures they would have together when he returned. He says maybe you and mom can come visit me in a couple months. Excited about the possibilities my mood became a little lighter. Maybe this will work out after all.

It was the 4th of July and my son brought me his phone to charge it as he always did. To my surprise I notice that my husband was still logged into his email account with new notifications. Driven by curiosity, I opened them.

Clicking on the most recent email an alert popped up to download an app to chat with friends. It was a picture of her. Should I? I trust him now and I really shouldn't be looking for stuff, but I couldn't shake the feeling. Accepting the download and waiting for the app to open not realizing I had just opened Pandora's box.

The app opened with hundreds of messages. It was an ongoing chat between my husband and the other woman. Although I was using his login I could see what he typed on my screen. Messages, pictures and plans for a future, very different from mines. She told him she was on her way and could not believe he came back to her. He told her, she was his true love and would never leave her again.

Trying to contain myself as I read the words on my screen. Getting deeper into their conversation. Pictures of him with her family, stories of how their lives would be together. Love letters he wrote saying how he would leave his family behind just to be with her. He talked of how he hoped that everyone would forgive him one day, but he made his choice.

The messages were beyond painful. Here it is a believed him when begged me to stay. Believed him when he told me he wanted to fight for his family. Believed him when he said he was done with her.

Scrolling through the messages I found pictures of his orders. He had the ship cancel them to be sent back to her. The whole time I was fighting a battle that was already lost.

Still reading the messages. Learning more than I

bargained for, the app gives me the option to join a video call. Enraged I couldn't hold back any longer, joining the call. It cuts him out and now I'm on the phone with her. You bitch! I gave you the option to be a woman and tell me the truth and you lied! I'm going to kill you and his ass too! She hangs up.

I try to call him, but my calls go in answered. He calls back and I now I am releasing all the anger I have built up inside! How could you do this shit to me? To us? You even had us planning to come out there! "So, you're making fake profiles of me", he asks? Trying to play on any emotions tied to love for him to escape from his faults. Thinking my fragile state in which he was able to manipulate for months could be done so again.

Somewhere strength arises, and I had regained my self-worth if only for that moment. Are you kidding me? You know damn well this is your account I see it all I have the proof now. I was so stupid to believe you!

I tried to screenshot as much as I could, but she had deleted the conversations. With his mother set to arrive at any moment still unbeknownst to the problems that plagued my marriage and stricken with grief and anger it was had to compose myself. She asked repeatedly if there was something wrong. Replying always, "nothing" to questions hoping to keep my secret under wraps.

To this day I don't know why I felt so ashamed. It was like I was the one caught cheating. I hung my head low and my spirits were way down. People always used to say I wore my emotions on my face and my friends and family knew something was eating me up inside, but they didn't know what it was.

For years my family looked at our marriage as the blueprint to success. We always were so happy. Where I lacked he was strong and when I fell short he was there to pick up the pieces. We had the house, cars and careers and we were living life for-real. My family looked at my husband as their family I with his the same. How did this happen?

As my time with his family came to an end I made the decision to let my son travel back home with them. Home alone with my wedding dress in my closet and wedding invitation that were never sent my drinking got worse. I hid a bottle in every room just to get through the day. Coming across the bridge one day I remember crying and thinking to myself I don't want to live anymore.

Asking God for forgiveness I drove my car to the edge almost going over. Swerving back in the neck of time only to hit the median in the process. I needed help, depressed, lonely and on the verge of becoming an alcoholic. Something had to give.

Checked myself into the hospital praying for some help and a clear mind. The doctors started me on some medication hoping to calm my anxiety. Counseling helped finally being able to talk about the issues that had cause this deep pain.

The doctors called my husband to alert him to my condition. They'd sent an emergency messages to the ship for him to contact the hospital. Days went by before he would eventually care enough to call. After days of therapy and a conversation with my husband the doctor told me, "your husband has no interest in coming back and we have to prepare you for life without him and I know that sucks".

I went to the phones and tried to call for myself. Still unwilling to except that it was over. He told me, "your trying to punish us!" I responded, "What? Punish who?" He replied, "Me and her! You will do anything for us not to be together!" Hurt beyond compare as I sat there crying I have been your wife and your supports system for 10 years and the one time I need you thee most, this is your response? You can't be here for me so that I can get better? The phone sat silent. No response was given, not even an answer when I called out his name.

My doctor was right I must think about life outside of his return. Since the day I fell for him I never saw us apart. Dreams of watching our children grown together and thoughts grandchildren someday. That was my future but now, what is my reality?

I was released from the hospital but still not in my right frame of mind. Afraid that my husband would conspire against me to get custody of my son I hit the road to retrieve him from his grandparents. Arriving in the early hours of the morning, my baby awoke with a smile on his face. Wrapping his arms around my neck and holding on for dear life. My son refused to separate from me. He placed his boaster and the passenger side and held my had for almost the whole ride home.

Crying as he slept, scared for our future survival mode began to kick in. During my drive, I called and made an appointment to meet with a lawyer at 10:20. My appointment was scheduled for 10:40am. My son looks me in the eyes and grabs a hold of my hand and tells me, "I hope the lawyer gives you everything you want momma". Taking a deep breath as I walked in the lawyer's office armed with pictures emails and text.

CHAPTER 13

Daddy's Gone

It was weeks before the next time my son or I talked to his father. It was like once he knew I was done with him he was done with my son. Always asking why he hadn't is dad called. I wanted to tell him everything I knew, but instead I took a deep breath in and said your dad loves you very much he's just going through some stuff.

For months this would be my reply to him. Then questions turned into nightmares. He was very close with his father and as a child I can only imagine what type of thought ran through his mind once the calls stopped. Awaken by my upset son, momma I had a nightmare! Ok baby, tell me about it? I never saw my daddy again, he left us! Tears rolling down his face I didn't know what to say. Still holding in all my pain. We think that kids don't understand their surroundings but later I found out he knew something was wrong long before I admitted it.

His stay with family and whispered talks, his abrupt return to me, the impromptu visit to the lawyer's office. The wheels were turning from day one. My son knew his momma, and he knew something was wrong when his dad stopped calling.

Breaking down and giving up my last bit of respect for myself I called her. Hello, you know who this is, can you tell my husband he needs to call our son! She seems shocked, surprised even. She responded, "is everything ok? Does he need anything?" Yes, his father! He hasn't called in weeks, I replied. "Ok I will tell him", she said. This would go on for months. He would only call when I would hunt him down. Calling his job, sending emails, or calling her.

When the call finally did come I had voiced my frustrations. "Why do I have to call your mistress for you to call you son?" His reply, "because you just want to talk to me and I don't feel like I should have to". Blown away by his response. I felt like I was always taking a hit but this one was for my son. I told him that if he called the phone would always be given to him. Telling him how he shouldn't have to be hunted down to be involved promises were made, surely to be broken.

Asking my husband to tell my son the truth sighting all the questions and nightmares "I need you to tell him! He knows something is wrong". His response, "I will when the time is right." Over the next few months it was always the same questions or nightmares prompting me to call the other woman just to connect with him. Each time she answered always promising to make him call.

By this time my sisters had journeyed to my home feeling that I was in need. Being close to your siblings can be a blessing and a curse. It's the knowing that something is wrong, and you guys need each other. They looked at me as the glue to our family and suddenly I wasn't holding anything together.

Keeping up appearances for them on the outside everything seemed to be fine. Surrounding me in my bed which had become my favorite spot in the house in intervention took place. What's wrong? Something has been off for months so tell us? I didn't know where to start. Just diving in I told them he cheated on me and he left me.

They all looked on in disbelief. Not wanting to think the worst of him. Some offering advice telling me how he's a good man who made a mistake. Still holding on to all the hell I'd been put through inside I just didn't want to tell them everything. My sisters stayed to comfort me. Focusing their energy on my son and me. It was a nice distraction from the pain.

CHAPTER 14

Low

Blow after blow, new revelations would reveal itself as time went on, but nothing could prepare me for this one.

Christmas Day and a post of a sonogram announcing to the world that she was expecting and how happy she was. I called immediately, "your pregnant?" I asked. "Yes, what it matters, its none of your business!" The once nice voice on the other end of the phone had changed into that of a hostile one. Is it my husbands? She hangs up. I call him. "Is it yours?" Nothing said. Again, I ask this time screaming "is it yours?" Yes, he said very quietly as he responded.

Another blow to head, another punch in the gut. A baby, something that I long for, dreamed of and here it is she's having his baby. It was then I hit a new low. It was rock bottom.

I tried for years to conceive after my son's birth without successfully carrying to term. I still had hope and dreams that my marriage would work. This secret just cut way too deep. I lost it and fell deep back into my depression.

In my bed tears streaming down my face my son came to my bedside asking, "momma are you still not feeling well?" Desperate for some interaction suffering from the only child blues. He said, "momma, it's Christmas. We're not going to do anything?" My son had no idea about the pending arrival of his sister.

Ignoring phone calls all day the pain I felt was like a

knife to the gut. Constantly making excuses sending him away he had been surviving on cereal and snacks all day. Noticing that I hadn't eaten he tried his best to take care of me bringing me a can of pineapples knowing that it was always something I was sure to eat.

I got up to use the restroom and he answers my phone, probably hoping it was someone to snap me out of the trance I was in. It was a coworker who was worried about me knowing about my pending divorce she had been extending an invitation to my son and I for Christmas dinner and had been looking for us all day. To my surprise it was 5pm I had slept Christmas away.

I'm sure my son was sad, confused and worried with no idea what to do after all he was only a kid. My coworker gave me pep talk and told me if not for anything else my son didn't deserve to see me in that state. So, we got dressed and set out to have Christmas dinner with friends. Still holding my secret inside. I tried to smile my body was present, but my mind was miles away.

The depression lasted for weeks causing me to miss work. I isolated in my room I would cook my son dinner and climb in bed telling him my head hurts. "My son would come to my bedside daily momma? Are you better yet?" It wasn't until I finally broke my silence that I began to get better.

CHAPTER 15

Lost

I felt bad for pretending that things were fine knowing my son could tell the opposite. Sitting him down I told him, sometimes mommies and daddies decide that they can't be together anymore, but they still love their children. They just decide to get a divorce. He looked at me very straight and with a firm look and asked, "does my daddy know about this?", he asked. Instantly tears started to flow. Was this question his way of blaming me? Does he know? He's the reason!!! In my head I screamed.

I wiped my tears and told him we both talked about

this and this is what's best. At this point I didn't know how to tell him about his sister. It was way too much for him to process all at once.

Lost with no identity I searched for someone to fill that empty void I felt. The only time I ever felt worthy was as a wife. Without that title who was I? He had moved on and found someone else and it was my turn.

Sinking to a new level of pain I found myself alone and afraid. Most of my adult life I'd been in a relationship with this man and I did know what to do without him. I found myself suffering from abandonment issues and wanting any man if I couldn't have my husband.

Desperate for a man's touch, compliments of my insecurities I craved someone to love since there was no one to love me. Away from the dating game for more than 10 years I sought out the help of online sites. Joining several sites with hopes of finding love so, I thought but it turned out that I was afraid to do the very same thing.

My loneliness fostered an unhealthy appetite to just be wanted. One site was for what people refer to as the "lifestyle" and it intrigued me. I honestly didn't know what this meant. I'd heard of swingers before but not this new thing. Soon I would realize that the definition I had in my mind was completely wrong. You see I thought swingers were just couples who dated other couples together, but my mind was blown to find out it was so much more.

Ultimately meeting a couple on the site, they would become my friends, my lovers and eventually the gateway to this other world. I would attend parties with them mostly as an onlooker until I would drink and lose my inhibitions.

After a handful of parties, I realized I was in over my head and would make up excuses to leave before the festivities would start or not even attend at all. Being a part of that lifestyle, I realized that I was losing more of myself. I was in a state of self-sabotage.

Little thought for myself, drinking, not working. Nothing seems to bring me any joy. I met someone through my circle of new friends and he befriended me in a way that I needed. He would come and cut my grass and take care of things around the house and eventually we became intimate.

Becoming a daily fixture in my life I began to poor into him everything I wanted to for my husband. He knew I was hurt and would allow me to talk about him for hours. This man was just content with being in my life in any capacity. He would offer to take care of me when I was sick. Rub my back when it hurt. Never pushing just taking whatever was given.

For months we snuck around because I didn't want my son to know about him. He would come to his games and leave before being noticed. I remember one day my son looking up in the stands and seeing him sitting next to me. He rushed from the field hoping to ask this man sitting next to his momma million questions, but he'd quickly left.

This man had started to win my heart maybe I can get over this after all. Eventually I introduced him to my son as a friend. Never allowing him to see us embrace or kiss I just felt that it was best. Wrapped up in the thought of having someone, anyone gave me the illusion of being whole again.

Spending as much time as I could with him I became addicted to the attention he gave me.

Always complimenting me on my beauty, my strength and his touch, it was everything to me. It was intoxicating. Despite not having my heart he gave me his and I felt bad for it. Feeling like I was using him, I'd always apologize for not being able to love him the way he did me. I began to shower him with gifts to ease the guilt. Whenever there was a need I was there to fulfill it. Afraid of losing the only thing that felt good in my life. I had to keep him in my life at all cost.

Soon my ex would be returning to the states and there was so much that needed to be done. Never filling for the divorce, I guess I felt like there was still hope. My friend encouraged me to fight for my family as he held me one night. Confessing that he had grown to love me but would not stand in the way.

CHAPTER 16

There is healing in forgiveness

As the months passed my ex returned home confusing both my son and I. Renewing promises made in the pass and now disputing the claims of the unborn child. Just as a began to try and move on with our lives he was back wrapping us right back up into him. This time standing in his committed more than he was before he promised to return home to restore our marriage.

Still visibly broken I decided to give love one final try as he return to finish his tour. Reestablishing my fight for my marriage I began to apply for jobs overseas in hopes that I could bridge the gap better with my son and his soon to be sibling. Several offers were made, and I was in the process of accepting an offer. It was during this time that the same behaviors began to resume, and we hadn't heard from him in weeks.

So desperately looking for answers I resorted back to calling her. "Hello, have you heard from my husband?" No, she replied. "If you do tell him to call his wife! Always meant with the same response, "ok I will ".

Although the calls to her resulted in communication in the past this time we received nothing. No more games, I'm done enough was enough and this time I was hiring that lawyer. Lurking on the internet again I found pictures of a newborn baby who resembled my son as an infant. This is when the decision was made to tell my son about his sister. He looked up at me and told me about how he wanted to meet her one day.

His remarks stayed with me daily basis, knowing that

one day I would make his wish come true. Bruised badly, on the verge of being broken many times before how I could deny this child his wish? I had no desire to meet her, but I'd try my best to fulfill my sons request.

With no idea how to pull this off. I wrestled with the idea for months. It was Christmas, a year to date that I decided to reach out to her only to find out that she and my husband had parted ways. We started to exchange pictures of the children even allowing them to video call one another.

Jokingly I mentioned my sons request to journey to meet them and to my surprise it was nothing but excitement for just mentioning the notion. It happened so fast I wasn't even sure if I would be strong enough to make the trip, but she insisted pleading for the sake of the children.

The planning began and once again I was a ball of emotions. This woman took my man! This should be my child! What's wrong with me? Trying to convince myself that my thoughts were crazed and deranged. So that I'd have a reason not to go. Who can say what I was feeling was right are wrong. It was my feelings. I mean, after all this is taking the term "blended family" to a whole new level.

Leading up to my trip I mentioned it to a family member of my ex's and the news traveled very quickly back to him. He was very upset, and it confused me. Having your children meet should be the goal for any parent you would think, so this caused me some anxiety and fear for my upcoming travels.

The trip was a total surprise to my son he knew we would be doing some traveling but had no clue about our destination up until our flight and the smile he had on his face was indescribable once he knew. My host had been gracious enough to offer her home to us, but I planned to stay in a hotel out of the fear of the unknown. Fears of the trip turning into an episode of sister wife's gone wrong.

The wife, the husband, the mistress and their love child all in one house, yeah it was deep.

We took our long flight in which my son talked about his sister 12 out of the 14-hour ride and it just made my soul smile. It continued to give me conformation that I made the right decision. Finally, we arrived at the airport and the greeting was one that resembled that of lost family members reconnected for the first time in years. She had tears in her eyes as she ran to hug and greet us. My son and I looked at each other as if we could read each other's minds. Joy! Happiness! Love! We both felt it.

The journey to her home was about two hours and my son slept well into it. She began to thank me for making the journey and telling me how much she appreciated my support for allowing kids to connect. I remember having mixed feelings about everything. We'd talked on the phone for quite some time and although our positions had changed we shared a common cause, we wanted our children to grown together and love each other nothing else matter.

The plan ride there, the car ride to her house, the wait for the child to arrive I was in constant pain, but I couldn't show it. My strength solely relied on the smile I saw on my sons face from the moment he knew this meeting would take place.

Later that day she would leave to pick up the baby and my ex from the train station and instantly I began to get nervous I didn't know how I would feel, what I would say. I hadn't seen him in months let alone the child he made in his absence.

My son and I slept and were woken to his father's voice and in a distance was a beautiful baby girl held by her mother. It was so funny to me, my son jumped up bypassed his dad and ran up to his sister as he looked her in the eyes and she reached out for him. In that moment I couldn't hold my pain any longer I wept like a baby. Tears uncontrollably, I didn't cause a scene just silently cried as they had their introduction.

The mother saw me breakdown and came to my side to embrace me, apologizing once again saying how sorry she was for any pain she'd caused. To compose myself, I wiped my tears away upset that I couldn't hide my pain from those who caused it. Everyone began to gather for dinner And I stayed behind. My son came back to the room and he gave me this huge hug and he said," momma, thank you letting me meet my sister. It was in that moment I learned to forgive. You see I had been searching for healing for almost 3 years, but it wasn't until that moment I forgave, that a received my healing.

After the trip ended their began to spout a friendship that no one would be able to understand. They would go on to journey to come stay with us for the holidays proving even more that blinded families don't have to fit anyone's specific mold. I think God for this ruff period in my life because it brought about growth and exposure to pain that I never truly dealt with.

The beautiful bond between my son and his sister will be natured and fostered for as long as I live. I am proud to call her mother friend and treat a daughter as if she was mines. I came through this Bruised but not Broken.

Printed in the United States
by Baker & Taylor Publisher Services